The Little Book of

LANGUAGE FUN

Ideas for simple language activities, linked to the early Stepping Stones of the Foundation Stage

Written by
Clare Beswick

Design and illustration
by Kerry Ingham

The Little Book of Language Fun
ISBN 1 904187 88 9

©Featherstone Education Ltd, 2004
Text © Clare Beswick, 2004
Illustrations © kerry Ingham, 2004

Series Editor, Sally Featherstone

First published in the UK, March 2004

'Little Books' is a trade mark of Featherstone Education Ltd

Published in the United Kingdom by
Featherstone Education Ltd
44 - 46 High Street
Husbands Bosworth
Leicestershire
LE17 6LP

Printed in the UK on paper produced in the European Union from managed, sustainable forests

Contents

LANGUAGE FUN

I n t r o d u c t i o n

Every child is unique and every child starting out in the Foundation Stage will have unique skills and individual strengths. Language development is absolutely critical to becoming an effective learner; so building early competency with language skills is essential for all children in the Foundation Stage, from their earliest days. The Little Book of Language Fun gives you the ideas to provide all children with a flying start in the Foundation Stage in the area of communication, language and literacy.

Children arrive with different experiences, attitudes and learning styles. The activities in this book aim to give the youngest children, and other children who need it, much practice and reinforcement of skills and competencies outlined in the yellow and blue stepping stones of the Curriculum Guidance for the Foundation Stage.

Using the activities with older children

The activities continue to be suitable for older children who need them. Some children who have had less time in the Foundation Stage, some may be making progress more slowly. You can use the activities for these older children as they are described, or you can adapt them by:

- ❑ using them in one-to-one situations with teaching assistants or other additional adults;
- ❑ making your instructions simpler, or more complex, depending on the group;
- ❑ encouraging children to concentrate for longer on the activities.

Using the activities with children who have English as an Additional Language

The activities are particularly suited to children with EAL, particularly those at an early stage of learning English. You can enhance the benefits of the activities for these learners by:

- ❑ using them in one-to-one situations with teaching assistants;
- ❑ involving dual language assistants or other translators;
- ❑ using the activities to reinforce new vocabulary;
- ❑ providing additional props and materials, including those from the children's own cultures and backgrounds.

Using the activities with children who have Additional Needs

Language Fun activities are ideally suited to children with additional needs. They can be incorporated into programmes for children in mainstream and special classes, and are particularly suited to those children whose learning is delayed or those who have communication targets in their Individual Education Plans. Most activities are suitable for one-to-one sessions, pairs or very small groups, and the structure of the activities enables practitioners to adapt the complexity and demand to the needs of the children.

Many of the activities also lend themselves to adaptation for individual interests, focus vocabulary and key skills. The suggested extension activities give you an opportunity to see how children concentrate, ask questions, work together and solve problems. These observations will provide you with key data for tracking progress towards the Early Learning Goals for the Foundation Stage.

The activities in this book give opportunities for children to:

- ❑ build two and three word phrases;
- ❑ use action and describing words;
- ❑ understand and use position words;
- ❑ use group words;
- ❑ understand and body part names;
- ❑ describe feelings and emotions;
- ❑ use words to describe size;
- ❑ practice listening skills;
- ❑ develop simple pretend play;
- ❑ build confidence in speaking to adults and peers;
- ❑ practice commenting, reporting, predicting;
- ❑ talk about home and family;
- ❑ increase their vocabulary.

The activities are enjoyable and varied. They are designed to make the most of children's individual learning styles and are clearly linked to the Stepping Stones and Early Learning Goals.

On each page, the aim of the activity is clearly described, along with the resources needed and what you need to do. Taking it further provides loads more ideas on each page, to extend the activity for more practice, to engage children with different learning styles and to move them on further towards the Early Learning Goals.

Language Stepping Stones and Goals addressed in this book:

Language for Communication and thinking

- ❑ ask simple questions, often in the form of 'where' or 'what';
- ❑ begin to build up a vocabulary that reflects the breadth of their experiences;
- ❑ begin to use more complex sentences;
- ❑ begin to experiment with language describing possession;
- ❑ begin to use talk to pretend imaginary situations;
- ❑ explore and experiment with sounds, words and text;
- ❑ extend their vocabulary, exploring the meaning and sounds of new words;
- ❑ extend vocabulary especially by grouping and naming;
- ❑ have emerging self confidence to speak to others about wants and interests;
- ❑ initiate conversation, attend to and take account of what others say, and use talk to resolve disagreements;
- ❑ interact with others, negotiating plans and activities and taking turns in conversation;
- ❑ interact with others, taking turns in conversation;
- ❑ link statements and stick to main theme or intention;
- ❑ listen to others in one-to-one or small groups when conversation interests them
- ❑ respond to simple instructions;
- ❑ speak clearly and audibly with confidence and control
- ❑ speak clearly and audibly, show an awareness of the listener by their use of greetings and conventions such as 'please' and 'thank you'
- ❑ talk activities through, reflecting on and modifying what they are doing
- ❑ talk alongside others rather than with them, use talk to gain attention and initiate exchanges, use action rather than talk to demonstrate or explain to others;
- ❑ use action rather than talk to demonstrate or explain to others;
- ❑ use isolated words and phrases and / or gestures with those well known to them;
- ❑ use language for an increasing range of purposes
- ❑ use language to imagine and recreate roles and experiences
- ❑ use a widening range of words to express or elaborate ideas;

- use simple grammatical structures;
- use simple statements and questions often linked to gestures;
- use talk for an increasing range of purposes;
- use talk to connect ideas, explain what is happening and anticipate what might happen next;
- Use talk to gain attention and initiate exchanges;
- use vocabulary focused on objects and people who are of particular importance to them;
- use words and/or gestures, including body language to communicate;

Listening skills

- respond to simple instructions;
- sustain attentive listening, responding to what they have heard by relevant comments, questions and actions;
- listen to others in one-to one/small groups when conversation interests them;
- distinguish one sound from another;
- show an awareness of rhyme and alliteration
- listen to favourite nursery rhymes, stories and songs;

Reading ad writing

- describe main story settings, events and principal characters;
- handle books carefully;
- have favourite books
- hold books the correct way up and turn pages;
- join in with repeated refrains, anticipating key events and important phrases;
- know information can be relayed in the form of print;
- link statements to a main theme or intention;
- listen to stories with increasing attention and recall;
- show interest in illustrations and print;

□ □ □ □ Mummy's Key □ □ □ □

Using two words together to describe possession

Group size:
Four to six children

What you need:
- ❑ Set of nesting boxes with lids
- ❑ Selection of small objects, such as pen, key, doll's shoe, tiny comb, ring, small cup and so on
- ❑ Music tape and player

T I P ▶ Try to choose objects that are of particular significance or very familiar to the children

---

What you do

1 Sit in a circle on the floor with the children and look at all the objects. Place one of the objects in each box and spread these out in the centre of your circle.

2 Ask the first child to choose one of the boxes. Start the music and pass the box around the circle until the music stops. The child holding the box at this time looks inside and tells the other children what is in the box. Encourage them to use a two-word phrase, which describes the object and its owner, such as 'mummy's key', 'baby's cup' or perhaps 'your pen' and so on.

3 Start the music and ask the next child to choose another box or beaker and then pass it on. Continue to play until everyone has had at least one turn.

Taking it further

❏ Ask each child to shake the box and try and guess what the object might be, before they tell the others what it is.

❏ When each object is revealed, ask the other children to think of describing words, such colour, size, texture words and so on.

❏ Talk to the children about object use, such as 'What might we use this key for?'

❏ Give each child an empty box. Ask them to hide an object from around nursery inside their box. Play the game as described.

Stepping Stones and Early Learning Goals

PSE: make connections between different parts of their life experiences

CLL: respond to simple instructions; use vocabulary focused on objects and people who are of particular importance to them; begin to experiment with language describing possession

KUW: explore objects

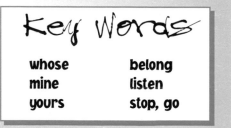

Key Words

whose	belong
mine	listen
yours	stop, go

A c t i v i t y **T W O**

Make teddy jump

Using action words

Group size:

Three or four children

What you need:

- ○ A doll or teddy each
- ○ Brush
- ○ Cup
- ○ Sponge, flannel and toothbrush
- ○ Small blanket

T I P ▶ Give each child a cushion or mat to sit on. It can help them stay still and focused on the activity.

What you do

1 Sit opposite the children holding your teddy. Make your teddy jump and say, 'Look teddy is jumping'. Sing 'Everybody do this, do this, do this, everybody do this, just like Ted'. Encourage the children to make their teddies jump.

2 Ask the children what teddy can do next. Encourage them to use two and three word phrases, such as 'teddy sleeping' or 'washing teddy's face' and so on.

3 For each suggested action sing the rhyme and copy the actions with the teddy bears.

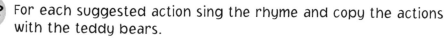

Next, take turns to choose one of the props and use this with the bears, such as pretending to brush teddy's teeth, with the toothbrush.

 Use the tune of 'Here we go Round the Mulberry Bush' and sing together 'This is the way teddy brushes his teeth ...'

Taking it further

○ Pass an action with teddy round the group. Such as, turn to the first child and make your teddy hop. This child then turns to the next child and makes their teddy hop. The next child copies the action and so on, passing the action around the circle.

○ Try this game of passing actions and action words around a small circle without a teddy or prop. Turn to the first child, clap your hands and say 'I'm clapping'. This child then turns to the next, imitating the action and the words. Continue this around the circle.

○ Look at picture books together asking open questions to enable children to use action words

○ Think together of a group of action words, such as action words to describe eating, such as licking, chewing, chomping, biting and so on. Try this with words to describe actions that fingers do, such as tapping, patting, clicking and so on, or perhaps action words to describe how a particular animal or insect moves – the possibilities are endless!

Stepping Stones and Early Learning Goals

PSE: have a positive approach to new experiences; feel safe and secure and demonstrate a sense of trust

CLL: use isolated words and phrases and / or gestures with those well known to them; listen to others in one-to-one or small groups when conversation interests them

KUW: talk about what is seen and what is happening

Key Words

doing	**same**	**more**
action	**again**	

Activity **THREE**

▼ ▼ Bridges and tunnels ▼ ▼

Understanding and using in, on and under

Group size:

Three or four children

What you need:

▼ Large trucks and cars
▼ Large cardboard boxes
▼ Scissors
▼ Tape

TIP

Get the children to help you prepare for this activity. It would be a good opportunity for children to think ahead and wonder together, such as 'Will the truck fit inside this box?'

What you do

1 Cut a tunnel in one of the boxes. Make a door in another to create a garage and open another box up to make a ramp, so that the cars can be pushed up onto the roof.

2 Play alongside the children taking the cars and trucks up and down the ramp, and talking about where they can be parked, <u>in</u> the garage, <u>under</u> the ramp, <u>in</u> the tunnel, <u>on</u> the roof and so on.

3 Take turns to ask the children where their car is, where it is going next and so on? Hide your car. Can the children describe its position?

▼▼▼▼▼▼▼▼▼▼▼▼▼▼▼▼▼▼▼▼▼▼▼▼▼▼▼▼▼▼▼▼▼▼▼▼

Taking it further

▼ Add some play people. Can you put three people on the roof, or perhaps two people in the garage and so on?

▼ Try this in the sand using wooden bricks and planks as ramps and tunnels.

▼ Take turns to hide one particular car. Describe to the children where it might be, using position words, such as high up, near the corner, far away from the ramp and so on.

▼ Use some small world animals with the boxes. Ask the children to place two zebras under the ramp, and one elephant on the garage, and so on. Give the children a chance to have a turn giving the instructions too.

▼▼▼▼▼▼▼▼▼▼▼▼▼▼▼▼▼▼▼▼▼▼▼▼▼▼▼▼▼▼▼▼▼▼▼▼

Stepping Stones and Early Learning Goals

PSE: display high levels of involvement in activities

CLL: respond to simple instructions; build up a vocabulary that reflects the breadth of their experiences; begin to use more complex sentences

MD: observe and use positional language; find items from positional/directional clues

Key Words

in, on, under	next to,
far, near	beside,
high, low	behind

▼ ▼ ▼ ▼ ▼ ▼ ▼ ▼ ▼ ▼ ▼ ▼ ▼ ▼ ▼ ▼ ▼ ▼ ▼

▼▼▼▼▼▼▼▼▼▼▼▼▼▼▼▼▼▼▼▼▼▼

* * Toys, clothes and food * *

Understanding and using group words

Group size:

Three children

What you need:

* Three small baskets
* Three small pieces of card and a pen
* Hole-punch
* Ribbon

T I P ▶ Look out for free recipe cards and leaflets in supermarkets for some clear pictures of food items.

What you do

 Sit with the children and talk about different types of clothes. Ask then to name some clothes items and draw simple line drawings of these onto one of the cards. Do the same for food and toys. Ask the children about their own favourites.

 Punch a hole in each of the three cards and fasten one to each of the baskets.

3 Talk to the children about what they might be able to collect in their baskets from around the room. Ask each child to find a few items of clothing, toys or food for their basket.

4 When the baskets are full, come together and talk about what they have found. Focus on the different names of each object, but emphasize the group word each time. Can the children suggest other items that they could put in their basket?

* *

Taking it further

* Try this activity with six children and encourage the children to work together in pairs.
* Play this game with pictures. Ask the children to cut or tear pictures from magazines and catalogues, of food, clothes or toys.
* Sort empty food and drink packaging, cartons and pictures into drinks, vegetables, fruit, fish, meat and so on.
* Sort a pile of dressing up clothes into clothes for warm weather and cold rainy day clothes
* Put the sorting baskets in the home corner for some independent play opportunities.

* *

Stepping Stones and Early Learning Goals

PSE: show increasing independence in selecting and carrying out activities

CLL: interact with others, negotiating plans and taking turns in conversation; extend vocabulary especially by grouping and naming; use vocabulary focused on objects and people who are of particular importance to them

KUW: sort objects by one function

Key Words

clothes, toys, food
same, different

few, many
sort, type, like

* *

Activity **FIVE**

☆ ☆ ☆ Tickle on the toes ☆ ☆ ☆

Body part words

Group size:

Two or three children

What you need:

☆ Clean feathers
☆ Soft brushes, perhaps a clean nail brush, soft make up brush, a new paint brush, a feather duster, a baby hair brush

T I P ▶ How about putting together a treasure basket of different sized and textured brushes for some sensory play?

What you do

1 Explore the brushes together using words and phrases to describe the texture and feel of each of the brushes.

2 Each choose a favourite brush and then choose a body part, such as fingers. Sing together '**Tickle, tickle, tickle on the fingers, tickle, tickle, tickle on the fingers**'. Encourage the chil-

children to tickle themselves on the fingers with the brush they have chosen.

**3** Ask each child how that feels. Swap brushes and choose another body part. With younger children start with just nose, fingers and toes, but make it more challenging for older children, finding elbows, ankles, heels, wrists and so on.

Take care that the children avoid eyes and don't poke the brushes into their ears or noses (or other people's)!

Taking it further

☆ Work in pairs with the children tickling each other. Let the child being tickled choose the body part.

☆ Ask the children to tickle body parts that you describe by function or ability rather than by name, such as something you use to hear, or perhaps something you can bend, or perhaps something you can wiggle!

☆ Play the game tickling body parts on dolls or soft toys.

☆ Pass a gentle tickle with a brush on toes or the back of the hand around a circle.

Stepping Stones and Early Learning Goals

PSE: have a positive approach to new experiences; form good relationships with adults and peers; relate and make attachments to members of their group.

CLL: use words and /or gestures, including body language to communicate; use simple statements and questions, often linked to gestures

body part words

tickle,	stroke	gentle
soft	firm	rough
hard	bristles	hairs
spikes		

CD: join in favourite songs, sing to themselves and make up simple songs

◆ ◆ ◆ ◆ Happy or sad ◆ ◆ ◆ ◆

Words to describe feelings

Group size:
Four children

What you need:
- ◆ Soft toy dogs and cats
- ◆ Blanket
- ◆ Basket and boxes as beds
- ◆ Lengths of ribbon for leads
- ◆ Bowls and brushes
- ◆ Pet magazines and catalogues with pet care products

T I P ▶ Try the 'Hairy Maclary' books by Lynley Dodd (Viking). They will provoke lots of talk about emotions and feelings, in a safe, enjoyable way.

What you do

1 Set aside a corner for some caring for pets pretend play. Play alongside the children talking about what the pets may be feeling. How do they let us know how they are feeling?

2 Try to draw comparisons with the way we express how we are feeling. How do we know the dog is excited? What do we do when we are excited?

3 Talk about what we need to do care for pets. How does that make us feel, how do the pets feel?

4 Join in with the children's pretend play, providing a simple commentary and building on their ideas. Try to get involved in their ideas, rather than directing the play.

5 Focus on words to describe feelings and emotions. Use open questions and wondering aloud to encourage the children to elaborate their ideas.

◆◆◆

Taking it further

◆ Make a happy and sad book, with a page of pictures and words of things that make us feel happy, and a page of things that make us feel sad.

◆ Think about everyday needs and feelings such as tired, too hot, too cold, hungry, thirsty and so on. Look at some pictures of babies and talk together about how babies let us know how they are feeling.

◆ Play a simple circle game of completing the phrase such as 'When I feel tired I like to ....' Always give children the opportunity to pass if they don't want to contribute.

◆ Read 'Peace at Last' by Jill Murphy (Campbell books). Go back through the pages, looking at each picture and talking about how the each bear is feeling.

Stepping Stones and Early Learning Goals

PSE: express needs and feelings in appropriate ways; talk freely about home and community; show care and concern for others; make connections between different parts of their life experiences

CLL: begin to use more complex sentences, using a widening range of words to express or elaborate ideas; link statements and stick to a main theme or intention; begin to use talk to pretend imaginary situations

Key Words

happy,	sad	tired
wide	awake	lively
sleepy	hungry	thirsty
scared,	safe	excited

• • • Same and different • • •

More describing words

Group size:
Two children

What you need:
- Two drawstring bags
- Two each of a selection of everyday objects, such as ball, shoe, keys, book, spoon, brick, sponge, brush and so on.

T I P ▶ Use pillowcases as feely bags for larger objects

What you do

1. Place an object in each bag. They can be the same object or they different ones. Give each child a bag. Ask each child in turn to describe what they can feel.

2. Encourage them to use phrases that describe the object rather than just labelling it. Ask them open questions to help them describe the size, shape and feel of the object. Can they describe it by its use, such as something you use for stirring?

3. Ask the second child to say if they think they have the same object in their bag. Can they each guess what is in the other bag?

4 Play again, choosing different objects. Each time, encourage the children to describe similarities and differences in what they can feel. Model the use of a widening range of describing words. Prompt them to elaborate on their descriptions perhaps by adding comparisons, such as 'This is soft and squashy like a cushion'.

Taking it further

● Use pairs of objects that are really quite similar, such as a tooth-brush and a nailbrush, a wooden spoon and a teaspoon, a bowl and a cup, and so on.

● Try sorting activities in small groups. Sort objects by attributes, such as size, or function, such as things used in the garden, or for washing etc. Talk alongside the children encouraging them to explain how they are sorting the objects.

● Create collections or treasure baskets of unusual objects to explore and describe. Try a basket of stones, minerals, shells and fossils, perhaps a tray of bulbs, seeds and corns, or maybe a seasonal treasure basket of objects significant to the season or weather.

Stepping Stones and Early Learning Goals

PSE: show curiosity; show confidence in linking up with others for support and guidance

CLL: extend their vocabulary, exploring the meaning and sounds of new words; use a widening range of words to express or elaborate ideas

MD: show awareness of similarities in shapes in the environment; use size language, such as 'big' and 'little'

KUW: describe simple features of objects and events

Key Words

same	different
similar	like
size	words
texture	words

✤ ✤ ✤ ✤ Big and little ✤ ✤ ✤ ✤

Size words in two and three word phrases

Group size:
Four children

What you need:
- ✤ What you need
- ✤ Washing line
- ✤ Pegs
- ✤ Assortment of socks, large and small

| T I P ▶ | Simple push-on pegs avoid the danger of trapping small fingers. |

What you do

 1 Fix the washing line at a height easily reached by all the children.

2 Sort through the socks together. Sort them by colour or pattern, such as all the stripy socks together.

3 Take turns to choose a sock and peg it on the line. Play alongside the children describing the socks you have chosen by size and colour, such as a big red sock, or a tiny white sock, and so on.

4 Ask the children to find a particular sock, such as 'Can you peg a big blue sock on the line?'

5 Encourage the children to use longer phrases by asking, 'I wonder who this sock might belong to?'- a man's big blue sock, or maybe a baby's stripy sock and so on.

�֍ �֍ ✚

Taking it further

✣ Add a pile of gloves to the game and ask the children to find an item, such as a small green glove. To do this they will need to listen for and remember three key words or attributes, the size, colour and the actual item.

✣ Add a simple washing line and pegs or a clothes airer to the home corner. Play alongside the children using two and three word phrases to describe what you are doing.

✣ Practice sorting according to size, such as all the big bricks in this box and all the small bricks in that box.

✣ Put together a treasure basket of pairs of objects, one large and one small, around a theme. A seaside basket may have shells, feathers, buckets, sand moulds, spades and so on, two of each item, one large and one small.

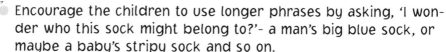

Stepping Stones and Early Learning Goals

PSE: be confident to try new activities, initiate ideas and speak in a familiar group

CLL: sustain attentive listening; respond to simple instructions; begin to experiment with language describing possession; extend vocabulary; especially by grouping and naming

MD: use size language such as 'big' and 'little'; observe and use positional language; use everyday words to describe position

Key Words

big and little
large and small
biggest   smallest
huge   tiny
long   short

▲ ▲ ▲ ▲ ▲ Listen! ▲ ▲ ▲ ▲ ▲

Listening and recalling key words

Group size:
Two or three children

What you need:
▲ Small basket or bag
▲ Collection of small zoo animals

T I P ▶ Make this game easier using familiar objects of particular significance to the children, such as their own shoe, soft toys, favourite books and so on.

What you do

 1 Line up all the zoo animals on the table or floor. Ask each child to choose one. Talk about each animal chosen in turn, praising their choice and talking about the animals.

2 Choose an animal to place it in the basket. Using the tune of the song 'I went to visit the farm one day' (This Little Puffin), sing:

> **I went to visit the zoo one day,**
> **I saw lots of animals on my way**
> **Which do you think I liked the best?**
> **Elephant, elephant, elephant!**

Ask the child next to you to find another animal and name it.

3 Ask the child next to you to find another animal and name it. Pass the basket to them to put the animal in as you sing the rhyme again together, changing the last line to:

Elephant and the monkey!

4 Ask the next child to choose another animal and name it. Pass the basket on and sing the rhyme again, the last line becoming,

Elephant, monkey and camel!

5 Put the basket behind your back. Can the children remember which animals are in the basket? See if they can recall which animal each has chosen. Check it out by looking together at which animals are in the basket.

▲▲▲▲▲▲▲▲▲▲▲▲▲▲▲▲▲▲▲▲▲▲▲▲▲▲▲▲▲▲

Taking it further

▲ Try this game with pictures, perhaps using the small cards from a lotto or similar game.

▲ Play a game of 'I went to the zoo and saw ...', each adding an animal to the list in turn and trying to recall the animals already chosen by other children.

▲ Make an animal noise for the children to copy, such as a dog barking. Next make two sounds, such as a cat meowing and then the dog barking. Ask them to listen then echo the sounds back to you. See how many sounds in a sequence they can remember!

Stepping Stones and Early Learning Goals

PSE: display high levels of involvement in activities; maintain attention, concentrate and sit quietly when appropriate

CLL: sustain attentive listening responding to what they have heard by relevant comments, questions or actions; extend their vocabulary, exploring the meaning and sounds of new words; listen to favourite nursery rhymes and songs, join in with repeated refrains, anticipating key events and important phrases

Key Words
listen
remember
animal names

✴ ✴ ✴ ✴ ✴ Give me a clue ✴ ✴ ✴ ✴ ✴

Using more describing words

Group size:
Three or four children

What you need:
* Assortment of objects from around the home, such as pen, newspaper, TV remote control, telephone, sponge, hairbrush, toothpaste, keys, spanner, sticky tape and so on. Try to include a variety of objects for different tasks in different parts of homes.
* Shoebox with a lid
* Blanket

T I P ▶ Use familiar everyday objects for children at earlier developmental stages.

What you do

1. Hide all the objects under the blanket. Carefully place one of the objects in the shoebox.

2. Give the shoebox to the first child and ask them to peek inside. Ask them to mime or pretend what the object is used for.

Allow each of the other children to ask a question about the object, such as 'Can you tell us what colour it is?' 'Is it metal or wood', or 'How does it feel', and so on.

 Encourage the child holding the box to use simple two and three word phrases including describing words to tell the children about the object. Prompt by asking open questions and modelling appropriate describing words and phrases.

 Give all the children a chance to guess what is in the box, before the item is revealed!

Taking it further

* Play the game with photos, pictures or line drawings of objects.
* Choose objects around a theme, such as a hairdresser, a doctor, looking after pets, the weather, a season or the natural world.
* Spread lots of small picture cards face up on the floor, perhaps from a picture lotto or pairs game. Pass the box around the circle. Each child in turn places a card in the box following your instructions to find say, something furry. When all the pictures of furry objects are in the box, let the next child choose another describing word to hunt for. Use colour, size and texture words as well as attributes, such as hot or cold, big or small.

Stepping Stones and Early Learning Goals

PSE: be confident to try new activities, initiate ideas and speak in a familiar group

CLL: simple grammatical structures; ask simple questions, often in the form of 'where' or 'what'; have emerging self confidence to speak to others about wants and interests; extend vocabulary especially by grouping and naming; use a widening range of words to express or elaborate on their ideas

Key Words

colour words
size words
texture   feel
guess   think

✦ ✦ ✦ ✦ ✦ At home ✦ ✦ ✦ ✦ ✦

Sequences of home corner play

Group size:

Two or three children

What you need:

Home corner resources such as:

✦ Feeder cup, spoon, bib and bowl for feeding dolls

✦ Flannel, toothbrush, towel and brush for dolls

✦ Storybook, tiny teddy and blanket for dolls bedtime

T I P	Collect old wristwatches for dressing up and try to find a toy clock and alarm clock in the home corner.

What you do

1   Sit with the children in a circle and pass the doll around, wrapped in the blanket. Tell the children that it's late and the doll is tired and hungry. Ask them what to do. Accept all suggestions!

2   Talk through feeding the doll. Put the cup, bowl, spoon and bib on the floor. Decide together what you need to do first. Encourage the children to suggest an order and to think ahead to the next thing the doll might want and need.

3 Prompt them to describe how the doll is feeling. Compare the doll's mealtime with mealtime routines at home.

4 Take the doll into the home corner and play alongside the children getting her/him washed and ready for bed. Comment on what the children are doing and model sequences of pretend play, such as washing the doll's face and drying her with the towel, before hugging her and tucking her up in bed.

5 Talk about time passing, model phrases like 'It's getting late', 'It's getting dark', 'I'm feeling tired'. Look at the pretend clock or your watch, talk about bedtime.

+-+

Taking it further

✚ Add some pretend curtains to the home corner that can be opened and closed, to indicate bedtime and time to get up.

✚ For a change in practising sequences, try a café in the home corner, or a picnic outside with a basket and a picnic blanket.

✚ Encourage the children to imitate and pretend play household sequences. Add dusters, a play vacuum cleaner and dustpan and brush to the home corner or to a simple den outside.

✚ Practice more sequences of simple pretend play outside, buying pretend tickets and going on journeys, washing cars and bikes etc.

Stepping Stones and Early Learning Goals

PSE: talk freely about their home and their community; initiate interactions with other people; make connections between different parts of their life experiences

CLL: talk alongside others rather than with them, use talk to gain attention and initiate exchanges, use action rather than talk to demonstrate or explain to others; link statements and stick to main theme or intention; use talk for an increasing range of purposes; begin to use talk to pretend imaginary situations

Key Words

tired	sleepy	hungry
thirsty	first	next
last		

▫ ▫ ▫ Alfie's shoe shop ▫ ▫ ▫

Using conventions such as please and thank you

Group size:
Three or four children

What you need:
- ☐ 'Alfie's Feet' by Shirley Hughes (Red Fox)
- ☐ Shoes, boots and slippers
- ☐ Shoe boxes and paper carrier bags
- ☐ Pens and sticky labels
- ☐ Calculator
- ☐ Till or drawer with pretend money
- ☐ Purses and handbags

T I P ▶ Try some unusual shops, how about a garden centre, fish and chip shop or newspaper shop.

What you do

1 Read "Alfie's feet" by Shirley Hughes. Talk about the children's own experiences of new shoes.

2 Set up a simple shoe shop together. Play alongside the children, inviting one child to be the shopkeeper and the other children customers and parents.

3 Encourage the children to use conventions such as 'Good morning', 'May I help you', 'Please' and 'Thank you'.

4 Prompt the children to develop sequences of pretend play and to focus on one customer at a time. Make sure each child has an active part, and is able to participate fully by playing alongside or by being involved verbally.

5 Encourage mark making to make price tags and receipts.

Taking it further

❑ Add a receipt book or an old keyboard to note down sales.

❑ Make some pretend bar codes on sticky labels and fix to boxes or the soles of the shoes.

❑ Measure feet with a ribbon and match this up to the length of shoes available.

❑ Encourage the children to use conventions around the exchange of money, such as waiting for change, handing over a receipt and putting change safely away in purses.

❑ Add a simple ticket numbering system, as found in most children's shoe shops.

Stepping Stones and Early Learning Goals

PSE: initiate interactions with other people; work as part of a group or class, taking turns and sharing fairly; make connections between different parts of their life experiences

CLL: use simple statements and questions often linked to gestures; having emerging self confidence to speak to others about wants and interests; use simple grammatical structures; begin to experiment with language describing possession; begin to use talk to pretend imaginary situations; know information can be relayed in the form of print; speak clearly and audibly with confidence and awareness of the listener, for example by their use of conventions such as greetings 'please' and 'thank you'.

Key Words

**please, thank you
your turn next
customer, sales person
till, price, change,
receipt, bar code**

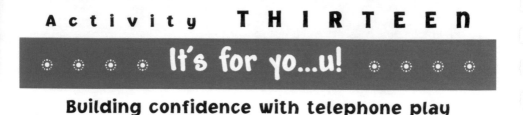

It's for yo...u!

Building confidence with telephone play

Group size:

Two children

What you need:

- ❋ A real mobile phone!
- ❋ Card or box
- ❋ Template on page 64
- ❋ Pens and children's scissors

T I P ▶ A huge cardboard box can be easily transformed into a telephone box – why not ask some parents and older siblings to help with the transformation.

What you do

 Spend some time exploring the mobile phone together. Listen to the ring tones, look for the numbers and talk about how to dial and end calls.

 Photocopy the template on page 64 and stick it on thick card or a small 'phone sized' box. Or you could make a phone by sticking round stickers on a suitable box. Help the children to add the numbers.

Help each child to tuck their mobile phone in their pocket. Pretend to call their mobile phones from the real mobile phone. Have a brief chat, encouraging conventions such as 'Hello name speaking'.

 Give them a chance to call you from their mobile phone! Have a chat about what they have been doing and what they would like to do next. Ask them who they are going to call next. You could pretend to look the number up together in the directory before they dial!

Taking it further

- Put together a display of all different types of telephones, telephone number index books, directories and notepads for the children to use.
- Add pretend mobile phones to outdoor play. Encourage the children to chat to each other and to you while you are outside.
- Try a children's karaoke machine in the music corner, or use the microphone from a tape recorder.
- Make pretend microphones and put with dressing up clothes for some pop star play and dancing in front of a long mirror.

Stepping Stones and Early Learning Goals

PSE: show curiosity; initiate interactions with other people; demonstrate flexibility and adapt their behaviour to different events

CLL: have emerging self-confidence to speak to others about wants and interests; use language for an increasing range of purposes; use language to imagine and recreate roles and experiences

KUW: know how simple equipment works

Key Words

telephone   call
mobile   dial
ringing

✪ It's broken! – fracture clinic ✪

Mark making and pretend play

Group size:
Four children

What you need:
- ✪ Bandages
- ✪ Lengths of ribbon or Velcro for fastening bandages
- ✪ Walking sticks
- ✪ X-rays
- ✪ Books about hospitals
- ✪ Notepads, labels and pens
- ✪ Black paper and white chalk
- ✪ Telephone and diary for booking appointments

T I P ▶ Give your local health visitor or the school nurse a call to see if they can help with resources.

What you do

1. Set up a simple hospital role-play, with reception area, a bed, treatment room and waiting area.
2. Play alongside the children booking in appointments, checking out patients and looking at X-rays.
3. Make your own X-rays, using white chalk on black paper.

Bandage up limbs. Fasten bandages with sticky tape, Velcro or ribbon.

 Encourage mark making to note down appointments, make the X-rays, write prescriptions and make badges for the doctors and patients.

 Sit in the waiting are with the patients and look through the books together. Ask open questions to encourage children to share their own experiences of visiting doctors or hospitals.

Taking it further

✪ Add some weighing scales and a notepad for checking and recording patients' weight.

✪ Add a signing in book to the hospital play area, and ask children to sign in and out with the receptionist.

✪ Old envelopes and cards can be used to note down or send out appointments!

✪ Ask the school or local practice nurse to visit in their uniform. Visit the local library to find out more about doctors, hospitals, and our bodies.

Stepping Stones and Early Learning Goals

CLL: ascribe meaning to marks; use writing as a means of recording and communicating; write their own names and other things such as labels and captions; use a pencil and hold it effectively

KUW: remember and talk about significant things that have happened to them; show interest in the lives of people familiar to them; describe significant events for family and friends

CD: notice what adults do, imitating what is observed and then doing it spontaneously when the adult is not there

Key Words
fracture	limb
bandage	receptionist
doctor	nurse
mend	bone
skeleton	

Picnics and parties – go stripy!

Offering, saying please **and** thank you

Group size:
Up to eight children

What you need:
- Paper plates and pens
- Stripy wallpaper or fabric for a table covering
- Bread, butter, sliced cheese, green apples
- Sharp knife for adult use
- Children's knives for spreading
- Red and yellow pepper
- Aprons and clean hands!

T I P	Grab every excuse for a party or picnic – keep it simple and help the children to plan and organise it.

What you do

1. Look at stripes around nursery – how many stripy things can you find? Explain to the children that you are going to make a stripy picnic!

2. Decorate the edge of the paper plates to give a stripy finish. Encourage the children to talk as they work, making regular patterns with alternating colours.

3 Cover a table with the stripy paper or fabric.

4 Make simple cheese sandwiches, adding a layer of thinly sliced washed apples. Encourage the children to be as independent as possible.

5 Carefully use the sharp knife to cut the sandwiches into thin fingers. Wash and slice the red and yellow pepper into thin strips.

6 Help the children to arrange the food onto serving plates.

7 Encourage all the children to sit quietly as they take turns to offer the sandwiches and vegetables around. Help each child with gentle reminders and prompts to say 'Yes please', or 'No thank you'.

8 Praise both the server and the children for sitting quietly.

Taking it further

● Try and include a picnic, party or similar in each topic you plan. Encourage older children to take care of new, or less confident, or younger children.

● Make placemats and menus and set up a home corner café.

Stepping Stones and Early Learning Goals

PSE: have a positive approach to new experiences; have a sense of belonging; demonstrate flexibility and adapt their behaviour to different events, social situations, changes in routine

CLL: speak clearly and audibly, show an awareness of the listener by their use of greetings and conventions such as 'please' and 'thank you'

Key Words

yes please and no thank you

your turn

stripy

pattern

straight

curly

Crunchy

crisp

Soft,

tasty

Healthy

✦ ✦ ✦ ✦ ✦ **Blow it!** ✦ ✦ ✦ ✦ ✦

Improving control of muscles

Group size:
Two or three children

What you need:
✦ What you need
✦ Clean feathers
✦ Tissue paper squares
✦ Mirror
✦ Hoop

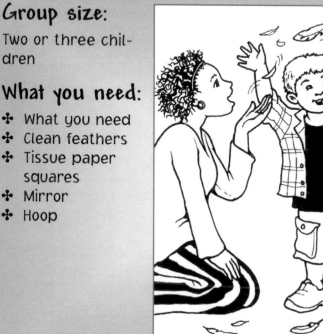

T I P ▶ Look in education catalogues, craft stalls and needlework shops for suitable feathers

What you do

✦ Look in the mirror and blow. Can you blow fast? Can you blow slowly? Try big puffs and then small tiny slow long whistles. Play alongside the children imitating their blowing actions and encouraging them to watch and copy you.

2 Place the hoop on the floor. Sit on the floor about a metre away from the hoop. Hold the feathers high in the air and see if you can blow them up into the air. Keep blowing the feather in the direction of the hoop.

3 Keep going until all the feathers are in the hoop.

4 Try the same with the tissue paper squares.

✤ ✤

Taking it further

✤ Blow chiffon scarves high in the air. How high and how far can you make them go?

✤ Try some bubble or blow painting with runny paint.

✤ Bubble blowers are ideal for outside play in small groups – make sure the bubble mixture doesn't go in eyes.

✤ Chalk a track on a table top. Blow tiny tissue paper balls along the track!

✤ ✤

Stepping Stones and Early Learning Goals

PSE: respond to simple instructions; build up a vocabulary that reflects their breadth of experiences; use a widening range of words to express or elaborate ideas; engage in activities requiring hand eye co-ordination

PD: initiates new combinations of movement and gesture; demonstrates fine motor control

CD: use their bodies to explore texture and space; show an interest in what they feel, hear, smell and see

Key Words

blow	puff
hard	gentle
big	small
long	short
sharp	air
high	low
lips	tongue
nose	

✤ ✤ ✤ ✤ ✤ ✤ ✤ ✤ ✤ ✤ ✤ ✤ ✤ ✤ ✤ ✤ ✤ ✤ ✤

▲ ▲ ▲ ▲ In the mirror ▲ ▲ ▲ ▲

Building confidence with dressing up fun

Group size:
Up to four children

What you need:
- ▲ Long mirror
- ▲ Skirts, shirts, trousers, ties
- ▲ Hats, socks, shoes and bags
- ▲ Sunglasses, hair accessories and jewellery
- ▲ Small pieces of card and a marker pen

> **T I P** ▶ Put a list of resources you need on the parents notice board.

What you do

1 Sit with the children and sort the dressing up clothes and accessories into groups: jewellery, hats, shoes, coats, etc.

2 For each group of clothing/accessories make a label using line drawings and a single word on one of the small cards.

3 Shuffle the cards and place them face down on the carpet.
Take turns to choose a card and find a matching item and put

Take turns to choose a card and find a matching item and put it on. Return the card to the floor.

 Keep going until all the clothes and other items are used. Admire each other's crazy mixed up outfits in the mirror.

 Encourage the children to comment on the different items, ask open questions and model appropriate phrases. Try to extend the way language is being used, encouraging children to question, comment, report and predict.

▲▲▲▲▲▲▲▲▲▲▲▲▲▲▲▲▲▲▲▲▲▲▲▲▲▲▲▲▲▲▲

Taking it further

▲ Play this game with clothes for different events and occasions, such as swimwear, party wear, outdoor clothes, wedding gear or builder's outfits.

▲ Play in pairs, taking turns to choose an item from the dressing up box for each other in turn.

▲ Put together a treasure basket of jewellery and small accessories including tiny purses to explore.

▲ Check for allergies first, then try painting small designs on the back of each other's hands with face paints. Encourage the children to talk to each other about patterns and designs first.

▲▲▲▲▲▲▲▲▲▲▲▲▲▲▲▲▲▲▲▲▲▲▲▲▲▲▲▲▲▲▲

Stepping Stones and Early Learning Goals

PSE: show care and concern for self; seek out others to share experiences; feel safe and secure and demonstrate a sense of trust; form good relationships with adults and peers

CLL: respond to simple instructions; extend vocabulary especially by grouping and naming; extend their vocabulary, exploring the meaning and sounds of new words; speak clearly and audibly with confidence and control

Key Words
body part words
mirror   **reflection**
clothes words   **jewellery**
footwear words

Three Billy Goats

Commenting and reporting

Group size:
Three or four children

What you need:
* Wooden bricks
* Small troll figure or other creature!
* Three goats
* Some green fabric
* Sand tray of damp sand

> **T I P** ▶ Singing a commentary is a great way to grab attention and focus children's attention.

What you do

1. Tell the children the traditional story 'Three Billy Goats Gruff'. Encourage them to join in with repeated phrases and refrains, such as 'Who's that trip trapping over my bridge?' and so on.

2. Help the children to build a bridge in the sand tray with the wooden bricks and spread the green fabric out to create the field where the goats want to graze.

3. Give each child a goat, or the troll. Play alongside the children, retelling the tale. Go slowly, allowing the children to develop the story or adapt it in their own way.

4 Ask open questions and encourage them to report what has happened, comment on what is happening now, and predict what might happen next.

 5 Listen carefully to the language being used and encourage the children to relate their play back to the familiar repeated phrases of the story.

6 Help the children to negotiate with each other and take turns.

Taking it further

* Build a pretend bridge, laying corrugated card to the floor outside. Trundle over it with bikes and scooters, repeating familiar phrases from the story.
* Provide props for other traditional tales to be played out in sand and water play, such as Three Little Pigs or The Enormous Pancake.
* Think of combining construction toys like Duplo with water play for boat building and other small world imaginative play.
* Add cardboard boxes to the train set to make tunnels, bridges and cuttings.

Stepping Stones and Early Learning Goals

CLL: interact with others, negotiating plans and activities and taking turns in conversation; join in with repeated refrains, anticipating key events and important phrases; listen to stories with increasing attention and recall; describe main story settings, events and principal characters; link statements to a main theme or intention; use talk to connect ideas, explain what is happening and anticipate what might happen next

CD: introduce a story line or narrative into their play; play co-operatively as part of a group to act out a narrative

Key Words

trip, trap
three billy goats
great big, middle sized
and little
over and under
bridge, troll

✦ ✦ ✦ ✦ All about me ✦ ✦ ✦ ✦

A treasure book - talking about home and family

Group size:
Two children

What you need:
+ Thick coloured card
+ Hole punch
+ Ribbon
+ Thin card and paper
+ Collage bits, scissors and paint
+ Magazines, photos and catalogues

TIP	A digital camera would be a real asset to your resource cupboard, but it is not essential for this activity.

What you do

1. Make a front and back cover for the treasure book. Add the child's name, handprint, photo if you have one, and decorate with sequins and other shiny, jewel-like collage bits.

2. Mount small sheets of paper on pieces of thin card, cut to size to be the inner pages of the child's book. Involve the children as much as possible in making the structure of the book as well as deciding on the page content.

3 Create pages together that focus on My family, My favourite toys and books, My friends, My day at nursery/school, My bedroom etc. Cut pictures from magazines, draw and photograph objects and events. Ask the child's friends and family to contribute.

4 Use more thin card to make a treasure pocket in the inside back cover. Tuck tiny notes, pictures and messages for the child in here.

5 Fasten all the pages and cover together by threading the ribbon through holes made with the hole-punch.

Taking it further

✛ Ask parents to contribute a page or some photos for their own child's book.

✛ Make a display of the children's books alongside baby photographs of each of the children. Use this as a focus for talking about growing and changing.

✛ Encourage the children to talk about their day at home, as well as their day at nursery.

✛ Play a circle game where the children tell you their first and family name, and perhaps the number or name of their house.

Stepping Stones and Early Learning Goals

PSE: talk freely about their home and community; have a sense of belonging; express needs and feelings in an appropriate way; feel safe and secure and demonstrate a sense of trust; make connections between different parts of their lives

CLL: have emerging self confidence to speak to others about wants and interests; begin to build up a vocabulary that reflects the breadth of their experiences; know information can be relayed by print; hold books the correct way up and turn pages; handle books carefully; ascribe meaning to marks; engage in activities requiring hand eye co-ordination

Key Words

family	home
favourite	special
treasure	

❑ ❑ ❑ ❑ Picture this ❑ ❑ ❑ ❑

Looking for details in pictures

Group size:

Two children

What you need:

- ❑ Individual photo-
  graphs of all
  the children, or
- ❑ Pictures of people
  and animals cut
  from a wide range
  of magazines
  and catalogues
- ❑ Scissors glue and card

T I P ▶	Look out for picture books where there is a char-acter or detail in the illustration that is present on every page.

What you do

1   Trim the photographs or pictures so that only the main subject is showing. Glue these images to a large sheet of card to create a montage of faces or people.

2   Sit alongside the children looking at the different faces. See how many faces you can find of children; people wearing glasses; people with curly hair, smiling faces etc.

3   Spend time looking at and talking about tiny details in the pictures. Look for eyelashes, earrings, teeth, eye colour.

4 Fix the montage to the wall at child height, so that they can frequently return to it, to see who else, or what else they can spot.

Taking it further

❑ Cut or tear pictures from catalogues or magazines to make other montages of food, clothes, toys, favourite characters, plants, animals and so on.

❑ Look out for a range of different types of illustration in picture books. Take time to study the pictures with the children. Look for and comment on details. Try to use a rich and varied vocabulary to express your thoughts and feelings.

❑ Fix an old roll of wallpaper, blank side up to a table top. Ask all the children to draw a picture on it and add their name. Ask parents and colleagues to contribute too. Mount the resulting montage at child height in the entrance to your setting. Add 'Can you find ....?' captions for parents and children to hunt for details together. Provide plastic magnifying glasses to make it even more fun.

❑ Make a collage of photos of all the children and adults in the setting, add photos of families, babies and friends.

Stepping Stones and Early Learning Goals

PSE: persist for extended periods of time at an activity of their own choosing; display high levels of involvement in activities; have a sense of belonging

CLL: talk alongside others, rather than with them. Use talk to gain attention and initiate exchanges, use action rather than talk to demonstrate or explain to others; begin to use more complex sentences; use language for an increasing range of purposes

MD: observe and use positional language; use size language such as 'big' and 'little'

Key Words

small	tiny	detail
look	spot	search
hunt		

⬡ ⬡ ⬡ ⬡ Missing words ⬡ ⬡ ⬡ ⬡

Enjoying repetition and familiar patterns

Group size:

Up to four children

What you need:

* Soft toy puppy
* Basket or box
* Blanket
* 'Dear Zoo' by Rod Campbell (Campbell Books)

T I P ▶ Let all the children stroke the puppy wrapped up in his blanket in the box or basket before you start.

What you do

 1. Introduce the book to the children, show them the title of the book and point out the author and illustrator's name.

2. Read the book slowly to the children, taking plenty of time on each page, opening the flaps slowly and emphasising the key phrases, such as 'too big' and 'I sent him back'.

3. After several repetitions of the phrase 'Sent him back', pause when you meet the phrase again and give an exaggerated gasp, to prompt the children to fill the gap.

4. At the end of the story, take time to carefully pass the puppy wrapped in his blanket around the children.

5. Read the story again, encouraging the children to name the animals as they take turn to lift the flaps. Pause to prompt them to finish each page with the repeated phrase 'I sent him back'.

Taking it further

* See if the children can remember which animal is under the flap as you turn each page.

* Put one of each of the animals mentioned in 'Dear Zoo', in a small basket, along with the puppy and the storybook. Make this available to the children in the book corner or to borrow to share with parents at home.

* Visit the library together and look for other Rod Campbell books, or perhaps favourite nursery rhyme books.

* Read Eric Carle's The Hungry Caterpillar (Hamish Hamilton) and see if the children can recall all the different foods that the caterpillar ate each day.

Stepping Stones and Early Learning Goals

CLL: listen to favourite nursery rhymes, stories and songs; join in with repeated refrains, anticipating key events and important phrases; listen to stories with increasing attention and recall; sustain attentive listening responding to what they have heard by relevant comments, questions and actions; show interest in illustrations and print; know information can be relayed in the form of print; have favourite books

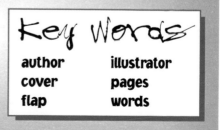

Key Words

author	**illustrator**
cover	**pages**
flap	**words**

✪ ✪ ✪ Whisper, whisper ✪ ✪ ✪

Listening carefully – a circle action game

Group size:

Up to six children

What you need:

✪ No particular
equipment

TIP ▶ Structure your circle time with a clear beginning, middle and end. Why not start by simply saying hello to each child individually and asking them to wave or say hello back. The game below would be the middle section. Finish with a favourite song or rhyme.

What you do

1. Sit in the circle on the floor with the children. Make sure you have their attention before you start. Ask another adult to come and help if needed.

2. Turn to the child next to you, clap your hands and prompt them to imitate you. They then need to turn to the child next to them and clap their hands, passing the action from child to child around the circle.

When the action returns to you, send it back again the other way around the circle. Next pass a short phrase, such as 'Good morning' around the circle, first singing it, then when the phrase has returned to you, sending it back around the circle, this time whispering it to the child next to you.

 Continue passing whispered phrases, perhaps a favourite character's name, or maybe a line from a traditional story or nursery rhyme.

 Encourage all the children to sit still and watch what is happening, even when they are not directly involved in the action.

✪✪✪✪✪✪✪✪✪✪✪✪✪✪✪✪✪✪✪✪✪✪✪✪✪✪✪✪✪✪✪✪✪

Taking it further

❂ Sit in two parallel lines, one behind each other. Starting at the back of each line, pass a whispered phrase down the line. Go as fast as you can!

❂ Sit next to each other in a line. Whisper the name of an animal to the child next to you. Pass the whisper down the line. The child at the end either makes the sound of the animal or pretends to be that animal. Check out if the whispered phrase has made it all the way down the line. Swap places and play again.

❂ For more circle time ideas, look out for Jenny Mosley's 'Here We Go Round', available by mail order from Featherstone Education.

Stepping Stones and Early Learning Goals

PSE: have a positive approach to new experiences; show confidence in linking up with others for support and guidance; display high levels of involvement in activities

CLL: sustain attentive listening; listen to others in one-to one/small groups when conversation interests them; distinguish one sound from another; show an awareness of rhyme and alliteration

PD: show respect for other children's personal space when playing among them

Key Words

whisper	quiet
listen	message
beside	next

☆ ☆ ☆ Be a pop star! ☆ ☆ ☆

Building confidence with microphones, music and dance

Group size:

Up to four children

What you need:

- ☆ Tape or CD player
- ☆ Dance music
- ☆ Long mirror
- ☆ Appropriate dressing up clothes and accessories
- ☆ Toy microphones, or cardboard tubes
- ☆ Musical instruments
- ☆ Foil or brightly coloured fabric

> **TIP** Make sure you have the time to listen carefully and check suitability of the lyrics on music and dance tracks that you have chosen.

What you do

1. Make a stage or dance corner with the foil or fabric as a backdrop, and the mirror.
2. Play alongside the children dressing up as pop stars and trying out dance moves in front of the mirror.

3 Agree mini-dance sequences and try them out to the music.

4 Let the children play their own music alongside the recorded music.

5 Talk with them about music they listen to at home.

6 Have fun together trying out different sounds and moves. Praise the children for getting involved, giving it a try and for their creativity.

Taking it further

☆ Why not make some cardboard guitars, or other improvised string instruments?

☆ Add scarves and large pieces of floaty fabric and ribbons to make for more imaginative dance moves.

☆ Make your own glitter ball, pasting shiny paper squares to a beach ball.

☆ Add some chairs, tickets and a programme, to make your own concert hall!

Stepping Stones and Early Learning Goals

PSE: persist for extended periods of time at an activity of their own choosing; be confident to try new activities, initiate ideas and speak in a familiar group.

CLL: initiate conversation, attend to and take account of what others say, and use talk to resolve disagreements; use language to imagine and recreate roles and experiences

CD: develop a repertoire of actions by putting a sequence of movements together; play alongside other children who are engaged in the same theme

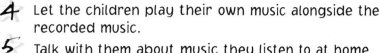

Key Words

dance	moves	swing
hop	jump	skip
beat	rhythm	

✦ ✦ This one is for you! ✦ ✦

Talking to adults and peers – making messages and cards

Group size:
Four children

What you need:
✦ Post it notes, or message pad
✦ Old envelopes
✦ Pens

T I P ▶ Have a brainstorming session to list possible resources and ideas for mark making. Get started with booking forms, till receipts, telephone message pads, memo sheets, index cards, birthday cards, parcel labels, and clip boards.

What you do

1 Give the children a real purpose by suggesting a message they might write for staff, such as 'Picnic in the garden this afternoon'.

2 Help the children to use marks, pictures and words to make a written message each.

3 Ask each child to take their message to a particular adult in the setting. Encourage the other adults involved to ask open questions to encourage the child to tell them their message as well as deliver their note.

4 Encourage the children to write little notes and make pictures for their friends and family.

✛✛✛✛✛✛✛✛✛✛✛✛✛✛✛✛✛✛✛✛✛✛✛✛✛✛✛✛✛✛✛✛✛✛✛✛✛✛✛

Taking it further

✛ Add a satchel or similar bag to this game. Encourage the children to write notes for other children, copying names from name cards onto the old envelopes and then play at distributing them around nursery.

✛ Copy the postcard templates on page XX. Colour and write little notes for distribution to other children or their parents.

✛ Add a signing in book to the milk or snack table, for children to 'sign in' when they arrive in the morning.

✛ Use chalkboard paint and a small piece of MDF to create a message board for the wall or cupboard doors in the home corner.

✛✛✛✛✛✛✛✛✛✛✛✛✛✛✛✛✛✛✛✛✛✛✛✛✛✛✛✛✛✛✛✛✛✛✛✛✛✛✛

Stepping Stones and Early Learning Goals

PSE: persist for extended periods of time at an activity of their choosing; initiate interactions with other people; form good relationships with adults and peers; relate and make attachments to members of their group;

CLL: ascribe meaning to marks; use writing as a means of recording and communicating; explore and experiment with sounds, words and text; begin to form recognisable letters; use a pencil and hold it effectively

Key Words

message	name
address	deliver
send	receive

✛ ✛

○ ○ ○ Funny voices ○ ○ ○

Animal and vehicle sounds

Group size:

Eight children

What you need:

- ○ Two adults
- ○ Blanket
- ○ Carpeted area, or surface suitable for crawling, creeping and wriggling on!
- ○ Plenty of energy

T I P ▶ Use a parachute if you have one available, but you will need at least one extra adult. Parachutes are often available to loan from your local toy library.

What you do

 Spread the blanket out on the floor, and sit around the edge. With the other adult and two children, hold the corners of the blanket. Pull it tight and hold it about 50cm above the floor.

 Explain that when they make a siren noise, like an emergency vehicle, they are to crawl under the blanket and out the other side. When they hear a train sound they must wriggle on their tummies on the floor under the blanket and out the other side. When they hear a car brrm-ing, they must go backwards on their backs under the blanket.

3 Practice each move separately before trying a sequence! Take turns with the other adult and children to make the vehicle sounds. Swap over so everyone has a turn to hold the blanket and do the actions.

4 Play again, with animal noises. Encourage the children to decide upon the actions and the noises to be used.

Taking it further

○ Use a collection of small toy animals and a bucket. Give each child a few different animals. Make an animal sound and then ask the children holding that animal figure to throw it into the box.

○ Give each child a different type of vehicle. Make a vehicle sound, such as a train. The child holding the train, rolls it across the circle to someone else. Keep playing with different vehicle sounds.

○ Play alongside children with farm animals in the sand tray, singing the traditional song 'Old MacDonald Had a Farm'.

○ Fill a shallow tray or cardboard box with narrow strips of tissue paper and cellophane. Add some small junk boxes for enclosures, and farm or zoo animals. Play alongside the children encouraging them to add sound effects to their play and talk about what is happening.

Stepping Stones and Early Learning Goals

PSE: respond to simple instructions; sustain attentive listening, responding to what they have heard by relevant comments, questions or actions; extend vocabulary especially by grouping and naming

PD: show respect for other children's personal space when playing among them; collaborate in devising and sharing tasks, including those, which involve accepting rules; move in a range of ways; go backwards and sideways as well as forwards

Key Words

animal	**sound**	**under**
vehicle	**listen**	

☀ ☀ Just the three of us ☀ ☀

Turn taking in a small group

Group size:

Three children

What you need:

- Three ribbons about one metre long
- **Compare Bears** in three colours (see tip)
- Drawstring bag, or spongebag

T I P   If you don't have **Compare Bears**, play the game with any other sorting toys or bricks that can be sorted by colour.

What you do

1   Help the children to lay the ribbons on the floor to make a triangle shape.

2   Sit a child at each corner of the triangle. Count the corners; count the sides, what else can you see that is shaped like a triangle?

Put all the bears in the bag, give it a shake and pass it to the first child. Take out a bear and place it on the first ribbon. Take turns to pass the bag from child to child, each removing a bear and placing it on a ribbon, all the bears of one colour being placed on the same ribbon.

3 Encourage each child to say 'Your turn' as they pass the bag to the next child. Begin to ask each child to guess the colour that the next child will pull out of the bag. Encourage them to direct their guesses to each other, not just to you.

4 Count how many bears there are on each ribbon. Talk about 'same', 'more', 'less'.

Taking it further

* Count and talk about 'How many more?' to be the same. Try guessing how many bears there are on a ribbon, then counting to check.

* Share a sorting activity. Give each child a red, blue or yellow bowl or box. Take turns to pull a bear out of the bag. The bear is then passed to the child holding the matching bowl. Encourage the children to use each other's names and conventions, such as 'Thank you'.

* Make repeating patterns with the different coloured bears. Encourage the children to work together, helping each other work out which bear is needed next.

* Sit at the corners of the ribbon triangle and take turns to roll a small ball or car, along the ribbon to each other.

Stepping Stones and Early Learning Goals

PSE: show confidence in linking up with others for support and guidance

CLL: use simple statements and questions often linked to gestures; use simple grammatical structures; talk activities through, reflecting on and modifying what they are doing

MD: use mathematical language in play; recognise groups with one, two or three objects; compare two groups of objects saying when they have the same number

Key Words

sides, corners	triangle
more, less,	same
your turn	next, again

✪ ✪ ✪ That's not right ✪ ✪ ✪

Using describing words, building vocabulary

Group size:
Four children

What you need:
- ✪ Doll
- ✪ Socks
- ✪ Soft toy dog
- ✪ Baby's bottle
- ✪ Railway track
- ✪ Car
- ✪ Two odd shoes

T I P ▶ For younger children, or those with additional needs, restrict the number of puzzling combinations to one or two.

What you do

1. On a table, put the socks on the dolls hands, prop the bottle up to feed the dog, put the car on the railway track and put the two odd shoes together as a pair.

2. Sit with the children and look at the objects on the table.

3. Encourage the children to describe what they can see. Talk about each pair of objects in turn.

Talk about what is odd or unusual about each pair. Encourage them to use describing words and to be clear and accurate about what they describe. Encourage them to use a wide vocabulary and to be detailed in their descriptions.

 Ask the children not just what is wrong, but also where should the gloves be, or what a dog drinks out of, and so on.

5 Encourage them to relate the objects to their own lives, such as 'Tell us about your dog', 'Does your baby wear socks on her hands?'

✫✫✫✫✫✫✫✫✫✫✫✫✫✫✫✫✫✫✫✫✫✫✫✫✫✫✫✫✫✫✫✫✫✫✫✫

Taking it further

✪ Let each child in turn feel an everyday object hidden under a blanket or cloth. Ask them to describe, but not name, the object for the rest of the group. Can they help each other to guess what is hidden?

✪ Pass an object around a circle of children and give each child the chance to use a describing word that tells us about the object, or simply pass it to the next child.

✪ Choose a describing word, such as hot, and then take turns to call out the names of objects that are hot - radiator, sun, fire, candle, match, cooker etc.

✫✫✫✫✫✫✫✫✫✫✫✫✫✫✫✫✫✫✫✫✫✫✫✫✫✫✫✫✫✫✫✫✫✫✫✫

Stepping Stones and Early Learning Goals

CLL: interact with others, taking turns in conversation; use simple grammatical structures; use vocabulary focused on objects and people who are of particular significance to them; extend vocabulary especially by grouping and naming; use a widening range of words to express or elaborate ideas; extend their vocabulary, exploring the meaning and sounds of new words

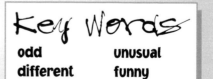

Key Words	
odd	unusual
different	funny
wrong	surprise

✫ ✫ ✫ ✫ ✫ ✫ ✫ ✫ ✫ ✫ ✫ ✫ ✫ ✫ ✫ ✫ ✫ ✫ ✫

• • • • • Sticky stuff • • • •

Fun with big and little

Group size:

Two children

What you need:

- Large card-
  board box
- Tiny box, for
  each child
- Collage and
  paint materials
- Scissors and
  glue

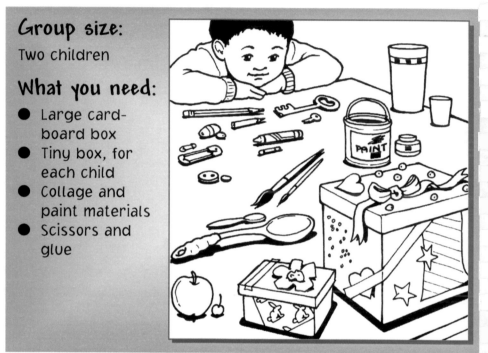

T I P ▶ Use your computer to make big and small
versions of the same picture or photo.
Stick these on card and use them to make a
matching game.

What you do

1 Work together to paint the outside of the big box. While it
dries, use paint and collage, shiny paper and sequins to decorate the tiny boxes.

2 Find some big pieces of pieces of paper and fabric to stick onto the big box.

3 Go round your room together looking for pairs of big and little objects to fit in the boxes - books, shoes, cups, bricks, hats, spoons, teddy bears etc. for the big box, and beads, paper clips, seeds, stones, elastic bands, coins etc for the little boxes.

Look at what you have found and compare the sizes.

Taking it further

▶ Cover a box with red and orange paper, and another box with foil and bubble wrap. Sort pictures of hot and cold objects into each box.

Paint some pictures of day and night. Talk about the sun and the moon and stars.

Make a texture trail with alternating rough and smooth fabrics.

Play a Simon says game of opposites, such as 'Simon Says open your arms', 'Simon says close your arms', 'Simon says go forwards, go backwards!'

Stepping Stones and Early Learning Goals

CLL: extend their vocabulary, exploring the meaning and sounds of new words; begin to use more complex sentences; use language for an increasing range of purposes

MD: show awareness of similarities in shapes in the environment; observe and use positional language; use size language such as 'big' and 'little'; order two items by length or height

Key Words
big, large
huge, enormous
little, small, tiny
size
bigger, smaller
medium
same, different

TEMPLATE

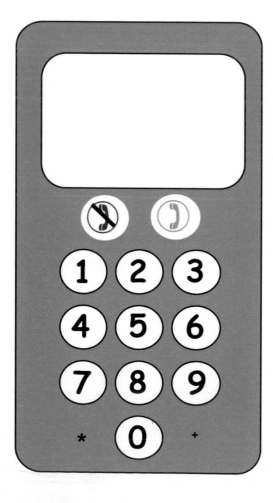

Photocopy this template and stick it on thick card or a small 'phone sized' box. Or you could make a phone by sticking round stickers on a suitable box. Help the children to add the numbers.